BLOCKCHAIN

THE REVOLUTIONARY POTENTIAL AND IMPACT OF BLOCKCHAIN TECHNOLOGY IN BUSINESSES, FINANCE AND THE WORLD

BY RICHARD HAYEN

Copyright © 2016 by Richard Hayen. All Rights Reserved.

This document is geared towards providing exact and reliable information in regards to the topic and issue covered. The publication is sold with the idea that the publisher is not required to render accounting, officially permitted, or otherwise, qualified services. If advice is necessary, legal or professional, a practiced individual in the profession should be ordered.

- From a Declaration of Principles which was accepted and approved equally by a Committee of the American Bar Association and a Committee of Publishers and Associations.

In no way is it legal to reproduce, duplicate, or transmit any part of this document in either electronic means or in printed format. Recording of this publication is strictly prohibited and any storage of this document is not allowed unless with written permission from the publisher. All rights reserved.

The information provided herein is stated to be truthful and consistent, in that any liability, in terms of inattention or otherwise, by any usage or abuse of any policies, processes, or directions contained within is the solitary and utter responsibility of the recipient reader. Under no circumstances will any legal responsibility or blame be held against the publisher for any reparation, damages, or monetary loss due to the information herein, either directly or indirectly.

Respective authors own all copyrights not held by the publisher.

The information herein is offered for informational purposes solely, and is universal as so. The presentation of the information is without contract or any type of guarantee assurance.

The trademarks that are used are without any consent, and the publication of the trademark is without permission or backing by the trademark owner. All trademarks and brands within this book are for clarifying purposes only and are the owned by the owners themselves, not affiliated with this document.

Disclaimer

All rights reserved. No part of this publication may be reproduced, distributed, or transmitted in any form or by any means, including photocopying, recording, or other electronic or mechanical methods, without the prior written permission of the publisher, except in the case of brief quotations embodied in critical reviews and certain other noncommercial uses permitted by copyright law.

TABLE OF CONTENTS

Introduction 6

Chapter 1: Intro to Blockchain 8

Chapter 2: The Impact So Far 12

Chapter 3: Understanding the Technology
(and the Necessity) 17

Chapter 4: The Implications of Blockchain 31

Chapter 5: Future Uses 39

Chapter 6: Arguments against
Blockchain and When to Use It 50

Conclusion 58

Introduction

Congratulations on purchasing Blockchain: The Revolutionary Potential and Impact of Blockchain Technology in Businesses, Finances, and the World and thank you for doing so.

The following chapters will discuss the purpose of blockchain technology and, likewise, the massive impact it's already had. First, we'll be delving into the history of the topic in order to give us a basic level of knowledge on why the technology exists and what its intended purposes even were. This is not an easy topic to tackle. It's very technical and it's very nuanced. There's also a whole lot to the history of blockchain, and the truth is that we aren't going to be able to even scratch the surface for the purposes of this book - not from laziness or anything of the sort but for the sheer fact that it's so intriguing and volatile that there's just too much to really go into within the scope of a book that's aiming to simply teach you the basics and essentially make a case for blockchain technology.

After we get through the basics of the technology such as the purpose and the history, we'll be talking about the nitty-gritty of the technology and its manifold uses. Heads up: there are a lot, even right now. There are only more to encounter too.

That will be the thing that we talk about after discussing the nitty-gritty and the uses, in fact; the numerous ways that this technology can be used going forward, and a few of the possible ways that it could change the world of business and finance entirely.

Lastly, we're going to be tackling the arguments against blockchain, and when it's really just honestly not a good idea to try to implement one. The truth is that blockchain is a revolutionary technology, but it's not always the best choice; there are many times where it's not even a good choice. I'm going to help you to identify those times so that you can make the most responsible choice for implementing a database however you need to, whether it be a blockchain or not.

There are plenty of books on this subject on the market, thanks again for choosing this one! Every effort was made to ensure it is full of as much useful information as possible, please enjoy!

Chapter 1: Intro to Blockchain

Blockchains are an absolutely revolutionary technology. They're the basis of the cryptocurrency bitcoin. Blockchain is essentially a decentralized way of keeping up with information - normally transactions, but it can be used for essentially any purpose.

A deeper description of it would be that blockchain is a decentralized technological ledger. It holds transactions and information on thousands of computers all over the world. The transactions can't be altered retroactively, so it forms a trust-based system.

We'll go a bit deeper into the exact technology that is powering blockchain in the next chapter, but the important thing to take away if, after reading this book, you only retain one piece of information about this vital and exponentially growing piece of technology, is that blockchain is a database which holds a public record of digital transactions.

Designed by a person, or group of people, using the pseudonym Satoshi Nakamoto, blockchains are designed to be the apex of anonymity and decentralization in the modern world.

The entire idea behind blockchain was designed alongside the cryptocurrency bitcoin when Satoshi Nakamoto identified the problem that digital currency was not nearly as nuanced as physical currency in that it required - until the development of bitcoin and blockchain - a trusted third party in the transaction as a mediator.

Blockchain was developed in order to remove any kind of mediation or trust in the process of digital currency exchange (and digital information exchange in general), such that the currency could stand on its own as a viable means of exchange.

The intent was to make the notion of digital currency exchange far more peer-to-peer and less bureaucratic in nature. In that aim, Nakamoto succeeded in creating a system that would transcend the notion of arbitrary third-parties in currency exchange and move past it in order to establish a far more egalitarian mode of exchange.

The concepts underlying bitcoin and blockchain were conceptualized long before the actual development of the bitcoin and blockchain technologies themselves. They have roots in other digitally scare cryptocurrency technologies proposed by bitcoin's early adopters such as Wei Dai's early concept of b-money and Nick Szabo's suggestion of bit gold

In its short history, bitcoin and blockchain have become immensely popular. The bitcoin project, alongside the first implementation of blockchain technology, was launched in January 2009 as open source software. Bitcoins are generated by mining, which is essentially verification of transaction blocks. There are rewards for verifying these blocks - fees related to the transactions, along with newly released bitcoin from each block. We'll get into the minutiae of these aspects in the following chapters, but what's important to note is that this is what incentivizes people to take part in mining bitcoin blocks.

Perhaps more impressive is the fact that the blockchain file for bitcoin specifically - meaning the size of all block headers and transactions combined - is around 90.6 gigabytes. Consider that every transaction is infinitesimal in size - at most a few bytes - and this number becomes massive. This means that this technology is a monolith for which there are few other words appropriate.

Another show of the technology's massive impact and huge presence is the fact that there are roughly 200,000 to 300,000 bitcoin transactions per day as of the time of writing in November 2016. Even a year ago, the average was around 150,000 transactions per day, and if we were to go two years back, the number is only five figures and is more along the lines of 80,000. This difference is huge, and the number is only going to grow as time presses forward and we find new applications for blockchain and bitcoin. It's worth noting that this is only bitcoin and that there are most certainly competing digital cryptocurrencies which have rather large bases of users themselves.

It's time that we stop doting on the broad concepts and get into the minutiae of the impact that it's had during its growth.

Chapter 2: The Impact So Far

Blockchain started with bitcoin and, though it certainly didn't end with it, it's impossible to really quantify the impact that it's had without thinking about the way that the two have intermingled. It's also important, in order to understand where blockchain is going, to think about where it's been.

For years, people in the peer-to-peer community had been seeking a way to get rid of the trusted third party in peer-to-peer transactions. We already talked about how Nakamoto put their theory forth regarding how this could be done. Nakamoto would develop it and send the first bitcoins - 10 bitcoins to fellow cryptocurrency enthusiast Hal Finney - and would continue to develop it for the next year as the community grew rapidly, before disappearing into the ether.

The bitcoin currency grew massively and exponentially. The bitcoin community was not without its demons, however, and it's impossible to talk about the history of blockchain and bitcoin without considering its checkered past.

Bitcoin offered a certain level of pseudonymity. This is to say that anybody can start a bitcoin address. This isn't innately connected to them and their identity, so there aren't any prerequisites and there's no direct link between a person and their bitcoin wallet. So long as they took means in order to prevent such a link from forming, it's feasible to say that one could use bitcoin with nigh absolute anonymity.

The anonymity, thus, invited the technologies to be used for less than noble purposes. Websites on what is called the darknet, the dark web, the deep web, or other variants of the same theme offered innate support for bitcoin as a mode of buying and selling illicit substances and products. You could have analogized it to having the same amount of inanity and impersonality as giving cash with someone on the street. As long as there isn't a way to link that cash to you, you're fine.

Perhaps one of the largest of these was the Silk Road. The Silk Road was the largest internet-based drug marketplace ever, by far and bar none. Also for sale were things like counterfeit money and unlicensed back-alley weaponry. This site met its end when founder Ross Ulbricht was sentenced and the site seized. Since then, certain people have found bitcoins synonymous with illegal activity. However, this isn't accurate at all.

Though bitcoin and blockchain did rise, without a doubt, partly because of their pseudonymity and resultant integration into the underground drug market, they were actually very in line with a lot of people's worldview. The decentralized nature of blockchain technology led to people from both sides of the political spectrum praising it. Free market libertarians, for example, were very appreciative of the fact that it disconnected money from any sort of banking monolith and got rid of the hierarchy of traditional trusted-third-party systems. Socialists and anarchists, too, were openly appreciative of the fact that it dismantled the power of certain monoliths in the world of online banking for the most part. Political moderates both to the left and right generally saw it as a great advancement in technology and a huge boon to the world of digital currency exchange, which became far more personal with the advent of bitcoin and blockchain.

Likewise, a great many powers have picked up bitcoin as a valid method of payment. There are, for example, a large number of foundations that accept bitcoins as a donation. Wikileaks are a fantastic example in this regard. Also worth mentioning are the Electronic Frontier Foundation. in 2013, Overstock.com announced that they would start accepting bitcoin as a form of payment. After that announcement, many major brands like Microsoft, Dell, Time, and Reddit started to follow suit and accept bitcoin as a payment method.

This is a weird way of saying it, since what really happens is that the companies accept U.S. dollars which are converted by their bitcoin processing partners. Regardless, the support for the fledgling technology is still very much there.

2014 was a rough year for bitcoin. However, the blockchain technology which powered it saw a number of developments happen in 2014. The largest of these was a development to the technology which allowed individuals with the knowledge and desire to implement a ton of new technologies.

One huge part of these was the invention of blockchain APIs. These allowed developers to build on top of the blockchain protocol. Also important, and something we'll be getting far more in-depth with later, are the concept of smart contracts and programmable moneys. These allowed a lot of the elements of risk with cryptocurrencies to be mitigated in favor of manually programmed exchanges. These have been used by companies such as Empowered Law in order to transcend what was formerly possible with blockchain technology, allowing the blockchain to be used in a much more intricate way than before.

One of the technologies building upon blockchain technology is called Ethereum, which is another cryptocurrency much like bitcoin. It has a much more nuanced way of utilising the blockchain, allowing smart contracts to be implemented super easily. Another perk of Ethereum is that it can be verified in a much shorter time than can bitcoin. Where bitcoin is normally used for transactions at large, Ethereum tends to be used instead for tasks suited to labor.

Coming third in market share for cryptocurrencies is Ripple, stylized lowercase as "ripple". Ripple also utilizes blockchain in order to decentralize current payment methods. Ripple released a blog post called Ripple and the Purpose of Money that discussed the history of money and how modern architecture for digital payment is bizarre and prohibitive. Ripple uses their architecture as a means to espouse the idea of instant release of currency. Their purpose in existing is to revitalize an industry that is currently clunky and hard to work within. They say that the state of current digital currency is reminiscent of the email of the 80s - a bunch of different providers have a bunch of different set-ups for the same thing, and if you want to go outside of that then you're doomed. Ripple wants to make this a thing of the past.

Bitcoin has also spawned a huge number of other competing cryptocurrencies, generally called altcoin (or "alternative coin".) The fourth cryptocurrency in terms of market share is one such altcoin, called LiteCoin. It is structurally and functionally incredibly similar to bitcoin.

The decentralized blockchain has lent itself to the creation of hundreds of different kinds of cryptocurrencies, many of which being direct bitcoin derivatives. There are now over 710 cryptocurrencies usable in online markets as of the time of writing. They differ in terms of minutiae, and we'll get more into the exact details of that in the next chapter after we talk about what exactly blockchain is.

Chapter 3: Understanding the Technology (and the Necessity)

As you can tell from its intense growth, blockchain is a revolution. We haven't seen the least of what this tech is capable of. Regardless, like any revolution, the bold and smart thing to do is to be at the forefront. In order to do so effectively, it's imperative that you understand what truly makes up blockchain technology and how it is implemented.

We've already covered briefly what a blockchain is, but just to reiterate: a blockchain is a decentralized database which maintains sets of records.

These sets of are called blocks. Blocks are, by design, resistant to change and modification of data contained. This is furthered by the notion of decentralized consensus.

The blockchain format is such that each block is, as we've said before, a set of data or transactions. Every block holds so many transactions. These blocks are hashed and then made into a Merkle tree.

Every block has a timestamp and a hash which refers to the last block in the sequence. This forms what is quite literally a chain of interconnected blocks.

So what exactly is a block? In its most common usage, it's made up of a list of unverified transactions. These unverified transactions are verified through the act of mining, which is running a specialized program that parses an algorithm in order to verify a block. Within the bitcoin system, a block is verified every ten minutes.

For a long, long time, there was a problem in digital currency. It was referred to as the "double-spending" problem. The reason that it existed is because there's an essential divide between digital and physical currency: physically currency has a clear existence, right? You can see it, you can hold it, you can hand it off. You can verify that money hasn't been spent by the simple fact that it exists, right there in your hands or pocket or wallet. This isn't so easy with digital currency, since electronic files aren't unique. They can be duplicated. Because of this, spending a digital coin doesn't remove its data from the original holder.

The main means of this before the invention of blockchain was by something called a "trusted third party". This existed in multiple forms. One could, for example, describe the company PayPal as a trusted third party in a way, as it acts as a mediator for financial transactions between two people.

However, a way to use and exchange currency without having a trusted third party simply didn't exist - and that was the big issue, wasn't it? "Trust"? There had to be a system which would absolve people of having to strictly rely upon a third party in order to ensure that a transaction as valid.

Well, it would so go that there were various ideas and concepts of what could be done in order to fix the problem of double-spending, but Nakamoto was the first to really cover a possible solution in detail and was certainly the first to implement it. It was because of the solid implementation that bitcoin even caught on.

The solution that Nakamoto came up with was called decentralized consensus, which we've spoken about briefly and only in broad concepts and big words. To dive a bit deeper into the concept of the "decentralized consensus", all it is at its root is the notion that we divide up the responsibility of keeping up with transactions, verifying them against each other's version of a block and then coming up with a consensus as to the most relevant copy of the block. This takes the burden of verification out of the hands of some third party and instead puts it in the hands of several different acting computers.

The key concept here is decentralization. That's the entire concept underlying blockchain and bitcoin, too - getting rid of any kind of firewall which would prevent the users themselves from having as much control as possible.

In other words: once more, necessity was the mother of invention, and it just so happened to birth us a beautifully mind-boggling system of innate checks and balances.

The necessity of such a system is found in the fact that it simply exists in and of itself. Trusted third parties are not a necessity. Think of it in these terms: the internet came along and decentralized information as we know it. Suddenly, everybody could take part within this system. The blockchain system allows people to take this third party out of the equation and do similar: decentralize trust and money much like the internet decentralized information.

I'd like to delve a bit deeper into the concepts underlying this technology though. For one, we need to talk about the type of cryptography which protects the blockchain. The blockchain has a specific level of protection which makes it incredibly useful and incredibly secure. This is essential to its decentralized nature. Because of this, anybody can view the blockchain but it's not open to security attacks.

This is actually absolutely incredible if you think about it because it means that there's a revolution of information and services coming up. But we'll talk about that when we talk about the implications of this technology.

Blockchain, too, is immutable. This means that it can't be changed or altered after it's been set to be a certain way, no ifs, ands, or buts. You cannot change a blockchain. It is a permanent ledger. It's like it's written in ink.

Blockchain, however, is not perfect. Nothing is resolutely perfect, why would blockchain be? Especially considering how fickle technology has the habit of being in the first place. If it's immutable, then what do we do when there's a problem?

Well, to answer this question, we first need to take a look at the two major kinds of problems we encounter with blockchain technology. The bitcoin project has actually encountered both of these problems and shown us possible solutions to both.

The first problem we could encounter is a major bug in the chain that causes something undesirable to happen. If this happens, blockchain can't be changed, but it can be rolled back. Rolling back carries the same definition as it does otherwise in technology: returning the state of a program or process to where it was at an earlier point in time prior to an issue. It can be likened to a system restore, if you will.

The first time this solution was notably utilised was in August of 2010. On the 8th of August, Bitcoin developer Jeff Garzik noticed that there was a major issue in block 74638. What he described as "quite strange" was that a block somehow had ninety two billion bitcoins. What makes this so bizarre is that bitcoin has a built in limitation of only about twenty one million bitcoins. Not certain if you're a mathematician, I'm certainly not, but that's almost 91.98 billion bitcoins too many.

What had happened was an issue related to the programming of bitcoin and blockchain. Computers store value in certain pre-allocated spaces, and these pre-allocated spaces are only supposed to a number of x size. If some kind of arithmetic occurs that makes this value exceed (or undervalue) that which is technically possible, it creates what's called an overflow.

Somebody, in an act of partial genius and total malice, realized there was an exploitable bug in the software that powers bitcoin. As a result, they presumably wrote a custom bitcoin miner which utilized that exploit and produced an overflow. What happened was that about 91.98 billion extra bitcoin was generated.

The community was at first confused, but after a brief review of the glitch came to the conclusion that it must have been a hacker exploiting a bug. The bitcoin quickly came to the community that the best option was to essentially perform a system restore on the blockchain to a period before the bug was exploited.

This was done, and things were restored to relative normality. After the "restore", a patch was released that would fix the exploit. This is one of the few times that a rollback of such nature has been executed.

The problem with this kind of solution is that it becomes exponentially harder with public blockchains as the user base grows in size. This was not too difficult back in 2010 when bitcoin was not nearly as massive as it is now. However, if it were done today, it'd be exponentially harder than it was before.

The issue, then, with such huge blockchain rollbacks is that a consensus has to be reached. A consensus is defined as 51% of nodes, in the example of bitcoin at least, agreeing that the blockchain is one way or another. In this day and age, with the massive number of bitcoin users, it'd be nearly impossible to orchestrate such a task. Not entirely impossible, however. A ton of chaos would be generated in the process, and depending upon how fundamental the problem is, it may not be able to be entirely fixed. If it's a small and obvious exploit, then it may be able to be patched and fixed. Depending upon the severity of it, however - if it were some huge and extremely obscure mega bug - it may not be able to be fixed so easily, if it all. It can be likened to economic booms and depressions - you can patch up certain fundamental problems that cause these, but the likelihood is insanely high that it's going to happen again.

The reason that the 2010 blockchain rollback went so smoothly is the fact that the user base was much smaller and the bug was relatively easy to identify and correct. These are variables that make a rollback very friendly and easy. However, had they been slightly different, it might not have gone anywhere near as smoothly as it had.

The second possible major error that any major blockchain has a pretty high chance of running into is a little bit more convoluted than just a bug. Because of the fact that blockchains follow a consensus model, it's possible that due to certain factors (difference in checking algorithm, different software, and related causes) that something called a fork could happen.

There are two different and distinct kind of forks which could occur: soft forks and hard forks. Hard forks are significantly more catastrophic than soft forks and demand immediate attention. Hard forks will often require a rollback, so they aren't necessarily a distinct problem. However, not all rollbacks are the results of hard forks, so it's necessary to distinguish between the two.

Anyhow, to define the two separate forks:

Soft forks are when block acceptance rules are restricted compared to earlier versions of the blockchain. These are forward compatible and don't necessarily demand immediate action, if any, because of the forward compatibility.

Hard forks are when block acceptance rules are eased compared to earlier versions of the blockchain. Hard forks are not forward compatible. Hard forks are much bigger of problems than are soft forks.

It's easier to illustrate these concepts than it is to necessarily outright explain them, so I'll give to you an example of a hard fork.

In March 2013, there was a hard fork, and from March 11th to March 12th, there were two distinct blockchains. A bitcoin miner that was running version 0.8.0 of the software created a significant block. This block turned out to be incompatible with earlier versions of bitcoin. As a result, people running version 0.7 were actually rejecting the blocks made by those running version 0.8.0. This led to an entire new blockchain being formed.

There was mass chaos and confusion for a bit. In the interim between the release of a fix, the bitcoin miners using version 0.8.0 were asked that they revert to release 0.7.

In an attempt to fix the problem, the primary developers of bitcoin looked into what might have caused the older versions of bitcoin to reject the new blocks in the first place. Soon after, a patch was released. Version 0.8.1 made absolutely certain that there would be no blocks created that could even possibly be incompatible with older documents.

This ended up solving the problem altogether.

Hard forks can be terrible for infrastructure. However, depending upon the nature of the fork, they could occur naturally as a result of the userbase. In the event that the users are unable to agree on a certain convention and move forward in order to fix the blockchain, it's entirely possible that two distinct blockchains could be used, and - depending upon the circumstances - both might even be considered relevant and correct by the community.

Those are the two biggest issues that blockchain technology will run into. That's not to say they're the only ones, but they're the ones to be most aware of. Any sort of decentralized peer-to-peer program is going to have some kind of issue with keeping itself correct and updated, even if it's purely in a theoretical sense and absolutely safe-guarded against in implementation.

While we're discussing the actual form and implementation of blockchain, it's important that we recognize that there's more than one explicit and finite form of blockchain.

There are two distinct forms and paradigms for blockchain: public and private blockchain.

Public blockchains are designed and created so that they are accessible to anybody who has the adequate technology to access them. Generally, this simply means a computer and the internet. Future blockchain technology of course may demand more, especially depending upon how specialized the service in question is. We'll talk more a bit later about how more technologies could come into play in regards to blockchain. It's impossible to overstate how multifaceted this technology can be.

Anyhow, public blockchains have multiple benefits. The most obvious is that it's truly decentralized because anybody can take part in it. There is no third party. This is what blockchain was developed to be.

There's also the fact that when multiple organizations use the same blockchain, it can cut operational costs by the use of smart contracts.

However, because of the open ended nature of blockchain, this isn't the only option, and thus private blockchains also exist. Private blockchains are blockchains which are only accessible by certain people or firms.

Many people, including many authorities on blockchain, argue that private blockchains are an effective waste of resources because it's not truly decentralized. If you know the people that are going to be verifying a block, then what's the purpose of instituting a blockchain in the first place? it's effectively useless at that point to go through such trouble, because the principal appeal of blockchain - the decentralized nature which opens it up to being transparent and not corruptible - is essentially invalid. At this point, it'd be easier and faster to implement a normal database.

Bearing that in mind, I'm not trying to say that there aren't certainly advantages to private blockchains. There definitely are. For example, the transaction speed of a private blockchain can be much, much faster than a public blockchain. And privacy is built into the private blockchain - it's the entire purpose.

For the most part, though, there's not much of a reason to embrace private blockchain, at least in my opinion. You're certainly welcome to disagree.

Having talked about public vs. private blockchains, there's one more major facet of blockchains which needs to be covered: smart contracts.

We've spoken in brief about smart contracts earlier in this book when discussing the history of blockchain, but we haven't talked about what exactly it is or how it could be used. Smart contracts are ways to add code to any given transaction.

Let's break this down. There's a tea shop in the town over from me. Every time you make a purchase there, they'll put a little hole in a punch card. Once you have ten punches in the card, you get a free drink.

Every purchase and transaction is a contract, legally and financially speaking. Let's say that this tea shop offered the ability to buy through bitcoin and only bitcoin.

Smart contracts would enable a digital version of that punch card. Every time you make a purchase from that address, it would give you one free transaction from the address.

This is a very barebones and simplistic example but what smart contracts basically are is a way to give much more nuance to blockchain transactions. There's a lot more that could take place with smart contracts.

For example, gambling is made possible through smart contracts. People could pay into a smart contract, and the smart contract would automatically pay out to the winner or winners of whatever was being gambled.

You could program a set of money to only work on a certain store. If you were giving a customer store credit for a trade-in at a game exchange or technology store, you could have it programmed so that the bitcoin that you transferred them only worked at your store rather than anywhere.

In other words, smart contracts are a way to make financial transactions, well, smarter. They're not necessarily an intrinsic part of bitcoin or blockchain. In fact, they err far more on the legal side of things than the financial. That said, legal talk and finance talk go hand in hand because money is the undercurrent of pretty much everything ever in our society.

Chapter 4: The Implications of Blockchain

So we've talked in brief about what blockchain is, but what does it really mean? We know the textbook definition, but what does it mean for society at large?

The biggest thing that blockchain means for society is decentralization. There are a million things that could arise out of decentralization, but the biggest thing that it represents decentralization of any given industry.

This means something very hazardous for the future of large companies. The thing about the blockchain model compared to the normal model for internet-based services is that the blockchain model is relatively impossible to track down. It naturally lends itself to any sort of peer-to-peer activity.

Think of it this way.

When you access a web server from a web browser, that server sends you whatever information it has to send you, which is then loaded and displayed within your web browser. If everything goes peachy then you'll type in the domain name, access the server via your browser, get information back, and be on Facebook or Google or YouTube or whatever in the matter of a mere second.

But what if there were an attack against one of these sites, or an official trying to take them down?

In the form of an attack, one could see a site be hacked into or its contents change. I can actually remember a point at which there was an insecurity in the web server of a government organization and somebody hacked into it and changed its content. So there's the first problem of a centralized copy: mutability. Anybody can go in there, theoretically, and change the content of whatever is being delivered from the server to the client.

In the form of seizure, one only has to consider the popular software piracy website Kickass Torrents which was seized by authorities and taken down within the last year. For a few months, where the site once sat instead was a sparse claimant page from the FBI saying that the site had been taken down for various reasons. This is where the second major issue with a singular copy and a singular distribution channel for that copy: fallibility. When you only have one means of delivering something and you only have one copy of that something, that something and that distribution chain are ripe to be seized. This example, of course, may or may not be controversial to even mention, depending on your stance regarding copyright laws and intellectual property, but this isn't the only manner by which a site could be claimed or seized.

The decentralized nature of blockchain and peer-to-peer technology prevents either of these from happening. It would be impossible to take down the entire blockchain network because there are multiple copies across multiple computers, it's self-replicating and self-referential, and there is little to no way that somebody could feasibly ever take the service off of the web no matter how bad they may want to.

There isn't a singular server for some zealous person or competitor to get a hold of, take down, and then completely ruin your business or application.

There's also the fact of the relative transparency of public blockchain. Everybody can view it but nobody can change it. This offers a lot of opportunities to actually, firstly, tighten up several processes in public administration and rid them of fraud, but it also allows them to make them free of corruption as well.

This could actually be a massive game changer in multiple ways that we'll talk about more in-depth in the next chapter, but right now, I just want to hammer in the concept of how important this whole notion is.

Transparency is going to be a massive reason that blockchain is used going forward. This allows people to know that something happening from person to person is truly supposed to happen, and allows one to verify that a transaction really did take place. The transparency works in the other direction too. Because blockchain is immutable, there is little to know doubt that what happened in the blockchain actually happened.

This is going to play a huge part when it comes to practical usage of blockchain technology because blockchain technology will allow the users to directly enter one thing or another into a blockchain and then it's on the record permanently, no redaction.

The fact that blockchain technology can be decentralized is key to what makes it so appealing for so many purposes. It's also why it could be a huge game changer and why so many people in the finance industry see it as a viable threat.

Blockchain offers the ability for people to quit having their hands held by trusted third parties and this or that institution; it allows people to finally be truly accountable for the things that they do and not have a mediary for any given action. This is why people love it. The autonomy that comes with it.

That autonomy scares people in power. That autonomy scares especially the finance industry, but also anything peer to peer that doesn't necessarily need a mediary party, because it could very well mean that it means the crumbling of said mediary parties.

This isn't too much of a concern at the moment, because blockchain in all honesty is still rather esoteric. The general person off of the street would be absolutely and completely lost if you asked them to explain blockchain and its uses. However, many things were once the same way. There was a time where e-mail and the internet both were incredibly primitive and only applicable to certain people. In fact, there was a time where even computers were primitive and hard to operate, and it wasn't that long ago. Before the Macintosh released in 1984, there wasn't really a consumer computer at all. But with that said, all it takes is time and the right platform to make something work.

Blockchain is going to change pretty much everything. The implication of blockchain currency is that we'll finally be able to get something that humanity has wanted since the development of the idea in the days of Athens: democracy. People are finally going to have much more autonomy over everything that they try to do and want to do. It's unnatural to have things be any other way.

Take currency, for example. The only reason that money goes through a central authority right now is because there's no other organized way. That's the long and short of it, to be perfectly frank.

Money represents something innate: value. Whether or not value is intrinsic is another discussion altogether reserved for late night talks of Marxist thought.

The history of money is so long and extensive that honestly going through the entire history of it is unnecessary and would take several pages to even give a proper cursory explanation. But here's the general way that money developed:

Money developed from paper receipts for stored grains. This would become precious metals which represented commodities stored somewhere. After a while, these precious metals began to have the abstract values of those commodities associated to them. This was the start of coinage. Paper money started in ancient China, and didn't hit Europe until around the 1600s because Sweden had so much copper that a copper coin with a decent valuation would be a few pounds and it was very impractical to carry around. Both paper money and coinage have carried over into our modern society, and were largely used to represent quantities of gold and silver and so on until the gold standard was largely dropped in the 1930s and 1940s during the midst of the Great Depression. Since then, money's value has become more of an intrinsic thing rather than a reference to the value of something else.

The point is that money exists solely as a way to give value to things. And for this reason, in order to have an organized structure of valuations of given commodities, we have to have an organized structure of money that can dictate such valuations.

This is the reason that every country has its own currency for the most part, but that these currencies are developed and distributed centrally: it's simply the best organized and most efficient way to keep a relatively orderly society with relatively well valued objects.

So the fact that we've managed to decentralize currency and move past traditional centralized distribution and organization of that currency is absolutely massive. It's impossible to overstate how fundamentally important to, indeed, human progress at large this could be if it catches on worldwide as a means of paying for things and determining values.

The implication of blockchain is massive decentralization, the likes of which we've never really experienced. I've said that this is the biggest thing since the internet, but if somehow a cryptocurrency massively takes off - if bitcoin continues to gain traction and becomes a predominant market force and eventually overtakes certain fiat currencies - if this actually happens, then it will be bigger than the internet. We've been searching since the dawn of civilization for a way to valuate things while retaining autonomy.

However, this also means a huge reallocation of societal power. A lot of people right now are benefiting off of the structure of fiat currency. We couldn't complain before, because it was the best option. The gold standard was dropped because it was a failure. Fractalizing the world's currencies and splintering them into more and more currencies that only work at this location or that location would actually serve to disunify humanity, despite the promises of free market types who say that fiat currencies are awful and a return to the gold standard is necessary rather than antiquated.

And the crazy thing is that despite this being such a huge step forward, there a lot of people saying that blockchain technology is overhyped. Like any technology, it has its limitations, sure. I'll be the first to admit that, humility being a key trait to any well-rounded person and all of that. But in my opinion, blockchain isn't overhyped. In fact, I'd argue that it's not hyped enough.

But perhaps I'm being overly optimistic with all of the "next step of humanity" talk. And if that kind of overtake by cryptocurrency were to happen, it would take a long, long time, and is unlikely to occur in any society where bankers have a lot of power because they have vested interest in fiat currency. With that said, there are a large number of undeniably amazing potential future uses for blockchain that can't be ignored. That's exactly what we'll be discussing in the coming chapter.

Chapter 5: Future Uses

Blockchain is a revolution. It's nothing short of a revolution. Once it comes into play and starts to hit the mainstream, blockchain is going to utterly and absolutely change everything that we know about finance.

In discussing the future uses of blockchain, it's important to recognize that not all blockchain data has to necessarily occur through a computer. The verification nodes may simply be run on computers, but there's no reason that anything else has to touch a computer.

You really have to think bigger than the current scope of technology.

Let's kind of break this down by industry in order to discuss possible future uses for the revolutionary technology that is blockchain.

Firstly, let's consider public administration.

One doesn't have to look far past any election to see that there are very apparent issues of corruption. Whether they're actual issues or inflated in scope and size due to the heavy emotional fragmentation and flaring which occurs as a result of elections doesn't quite matter. What leads to this worry in the first place is the overall lack of trust in the voting system and the feeling that it very well could be rigged.

This is actually the perfect job for blockchain technology. Because of its innate immutability and transparency, there's the possibility that blockchain could and would absolutely revolutionize the entire notion of voting and make it a far more transparent and altogether real process. This would work in parallel with politics to make people feel like it's less of a rigged game where the winners are already selected, thus getting more people to vote and be politically active in the first place.

Let's consider voting as a whole. There are different ways to implement voting. The most common manners are first-past-the-post and instant-runoff voting. Many people consider instant-runoff voting to be the most democratic but that's an argument for another book entirely.

How could we implement such a system? What would it even entail? Well, the blockchain would act as a ledger of every vote cast. Every time a vote was cast it would become part of a block. This block would be sent to the verifying nodes which would verify a block in set intervals. For this example, let's go ahead and use a federal election. Considering there are three hundred million people in the United States, let's assume a quarter of them are voting age and will vote at all. This gives us about 75 million individuals. Of course there are things like early voting but this is still a large load to bear for any system. Let's say that we verify a block every hour.

Every vote which is cast would be linked to a person somehow. The United States already has the infrastructure for this, in that every citizen has a social security number. We could use this social security number in order to link a vote to an identifier. However, these could be algorithmically hashed such that the information couldn't be traced back to the original holder of the social security number. This is important for protecting members of fringe political parties. For example, somebody who voted for the Communist Party USA or Party for Socialism and Liberation very well may not want their social security number linked to their voting preference because they could be put on a list or registry. This would function similarly to storing hashed passwords in a database.

Casting a vote would also work similarly to entering a password in a form submission: you enter your social security number and your vote is then linked to that number. This mitigates any chance at all of double-voting.

The social security numbers could be verified against a database to ensure that they exist. This may per necessity be checked against a centralized database of social security numbers in the U.S., but this already exists. There also may be an alternative method employed. The how and why of this doesn't matter too much for the purposes of conjecturing in this book .This is all just shooting at the stars in vague ideas of how this amazing blockchain technology could be utilized.

Anyway, every vote would be sent to the blockchain with a hashed identity. In this way, the blockchain becomes sort of a living, breathing "dictionary", to use a programming term. In programming, a dictionary is a set of keys and maps. The name is inspired by, well, dictionaries. In a dictionary, the key "apple" would map to the value of "a round fruit of a rose family tree, typically having a thin red or green skin." In our blockchain, the key would be a user's hashed social security number (or whatever) which would link to the value of their voting preferences.

Since a block is verified every hour, we would also mitigate the problem of vote counting and be able to get real-time election results. The blocks would be checked against one another every hour and then a consensus would be reached. This would be added to an election's blockchain.

For the purposes of efficiency and clarity, every particular sub-election within a main election may have a different blockchain. For example, the votes for a federal president in Wisconsin would go to a Wisconsin federal blockchain, which would then be verified and the values of which sent to the primary federal blockchain, which would then be verified. Meanwhile, the votes for the governor of Wisconsin would go to the Wisconsin state blockchain. This isn't 100% necessary but it would make it a much cleaner and more efficient system in the end.

I can imagine two ways to assure that you would have verification nodes among the general population. The first is to either pass legislation which actively enforces that internet service providers require their computer-owning customers to take part in the verification of the blockchains, or incentivize them to do the same. The second is to offer a federal stipend for people who are willing to use their computing power to verify blockchains. This would attract a great number of people because, frankly, who doesn't want an extra buck?

The key here is getting as many verification nodes as possible so that we have as many people verifying the blocks against each other as possible.

The advantages of this system are manifold. The first is that people would no longer be required to go to a voting location. So long as they've got a social security number (or whatever identifier that the system utilizes), they can reasonably cast their vote from anywhere: a home computer, a smartphone, a tablet, or even a library or a friend's laptop. This would heighten voter participation in the first place and get people to be more politically active than they would be otherwise. This would also enable people who don't have much time or freedom to go out and vote to ensure that they can.

This system would also reduce the chance of corruption, quite possibly to zero. All results would be verifiable by the general public if this were done by way of a public blockchain. Anyone tech savvy enough can look at every single vote that's cast, and anyone who cares enough to make sure their vote was counted correctly can find their vote in the public record.

This would be absolutely huge for public administration. It would completely alter the way that people view elections and make people feel much more connected to the political equation.

However, it goes beyond public administration. The blockchain can and will change the world of business, too.

A great many people have recognized the potential applications of blockchain for business. Blockchain integrates perfectly with the notions of a sharing economy, as well as the idea of an "internet of things". Before we talk about how it can be used for business, let's actually talk about these concepts and how blockchain integrates into them, because they're major concepts and they're certainly going to be coming up a lot more in discussions of blockchain in the near future.

The idea of a sharing economy is the relatively new idea that the internet be used for people to offer personal assets for certain services in lieu of traditional structures entirely dedicated to providing the same service.

Two prominent examples of sharing economies would be Uber and Airbnb.

Uber allows anybody with a license and a car to be a driver (with certain qualifications, of course.) This works great as a replacement to traditional taxi services because it allows anybody to do it, and not just somebody employed at a taxi service. Anybody wanting to make a quick dollar can do a few Uber drives.

Airbnb functions similarly, but instead of driving people around, people offer to host people in their homes. The idea is that they function differently to hotels because anybody with a home can host somebody, and it's no longer exclusive to the magnates within the hotel sector.

Blockchain integrates perfectly into the sharing economy because it's naturally geared towards peer to peer services.

In fact, a blockchain alternative to Uber already exists. It's called LaZooz. It's a ride sharing platform much like Uber, but it's completely decentralized. It's based around a currency called LaZooz. It rewards drivers, users, and miners with tokens called Zooz which can be used in order to receive rides.

And there's also more than one. Arcade City is another blockchain based ridesharing solution. It functions similarly to Uber, Lyft, and LaZooz. It has its own cryptocurrency as well, called "arcade tokens."

Now, on to the clunky concept of the "internet of things". It's actually relatively simple, but the name is clunky, so therein it's clunky, right? Anyway, the "internet of things". The idea of the "internet of things" is that anything and everything can theoretically be made to communicate with one another and network against each other.

Let's take your kitchen, for instance. Think about your fridge. Your fridge could very much be smarter than it is right now. At the moment, you have to double check your expiry dates, think about what you can cook based off of what you have available, go to the grocery store when you run out of a certain object, and so on. You have to actively think about all of these things. The "internet of things" says "no, these things should all be interconnected and talk to each other. This should be simpler."

But a future fridge - and this sounds like something out of the Jetsons, I promise it's not - could theoretically keep tabs on a lot of this for you. Your cartons of eggs and gallons of milk could have RFID tags on them as opposed to barcodes, and these RFID tags could communicate with the fridge and give it updates and information about the product.

Your fridge could then know what's inside of it. It could say to you "hey, you've got chicken broth, pasta, and uncooked chicken breast. You could make some absolutely killer chicken noodle soup right about now," and what's more is that it'd be right, because the internet of things would allow it to keep tabs on all of this.

Or maybe your alarm clock could be linked to your coffee pot. When your alarm goes off, your coffee is already either ready or brewing. The internet of things is based around the idea that everything can be a little bit smarter and that the objects in your house can talk to one another.

In other words, it's the future. We're already seeing it manifest in certain ways. Consider Tesla cars. Tesla cars automatically download updates to provide new features and keep autopilot driving up to date.

The problem with this model right now is that these things will have to be identified and authenticated through cloud servers in a centralized manner, even if they're right next to each other. There are two possible solutions to this.

The first still requires centralization in a manner, but it's localized centralization. Instead of having every object connect to the cloud and then communicate with one another from there, it's feasible that there could instead be a local server within a house that every object could connect to and that thus could instead be the protocol by which these hypothetical objects spoke to one another. But firstly, that's an additional expense. There's also the caveat that if that server fails or fries, then your internet of things is virtually useless.

That's one thing we haven't really talked too much about, but that's one major appeal of blockchain: if one node fails, the entire thing doesn't go down. There are still several nodes in possession of the blockchain and that are actively verifying blocks. I simply becomes like that node didn't exist. The load and processes are adjusted, and life goes on, either without that node completely or until it returns and starts taking an active part in the verification of the blockchain once more.

Anyhow, if we're aiming to avoid the caveat of a centralized local server connection, then this is where blockchain comes into play. In its traditional manner, blockchain will allow these concepts to be decentralized and act as independent units that can connect and interact without having to be going through a centralized cloud server. This is a really big deal because this will massively simplify the way that the internet of things can manifest and also remove any element of third parties from the equation, even if this hypothetical third party is just a little white box with a processor and a touchscreen through which all of your "smart devices" connect.

This actually became a bit of a tangent, but the point I was trying to illustrate is that through the fact that it can impact and possibly override in many ways the quickly-growing "sharing economy", blockchain will revolutionize the world of business.

There are no shortage of ways that blockchain could change the worlds of business and finance as we know them. Blockchain, as potentially innovative as it could be though, does come with its fair share of drawbacks and potential limits. It's because of this that it's necessary to proceed with a fair amount of optimistic caution. These limitations are exactly what we're going to be covering in the following chapter.

Chapter 6: Arguments Against Blockchain and When to Use It

This chapter is actually going to cover the negatives of blockchain, and places where it doesn't have applications, or where the benefits of blockchain are essentially nil compared to more traditional methods of storing data such as information databases.

Throughout this book, I've been building blockchain up, but it's not at all a snake oil. It's not a fix-all for problems in technology, and it's not going to take over everything in one fell swoop. No, in fact - there are quite a few reasons why one shouldn't use blockchain, and quite a few instances where there's little to no advantage to using it in the first place.

The largest disadvantage to blockchain is that its transparency also comes with an innate cost. This could be a reason that it may never completely supplant the financial industry or usurp the current role of currency in our society.

The reason that the transparency could also be a liability is that, while it may reduce the probability of financial fraud, it opens up a window of opportunity for cybercriminals. This window of opportunity very well could be used in order to take advantage of the public financial information and exploit it and wreak havoc in general.

But beyond this, there are numerous other disadvantages.

One huge one is scalability. This is to say that we don't yet know how suitable blockchain is for high-volume trading. Consider the current state of bitcoin. Bitcoin isn't actually that big of a currency in a globally relative sort of way. But even at its current size and its current state, it requires a massive amount of processing power in order to be functional. A blockchain size is infinitely growing, and the fact that copies/updates of the blockchain are given to so many parties can actually be a bit of a stopgap in discussions about blockchain scalability. It will become so big that it's unwieldy or even impossible to continue developing.

Add on top of this the fact that one of the main appeals of blockchains is the fact that they're decentralized, and you have to recognize that a lot of the processing nodes aren't going to be running on supercomputers. They're going to be run on ordinary computers like yours or mine, and this means that if it's going to be meaningfully decentralized, there are only so many transactions which can take place in a given set of time and be verified because otherwise, these machines simply won't be able to handle the burden of the blockchain in terms of volume and complexity.

There's also the major hurdle that blockchains are kind of massive question marks when it comes to the legality of them in terms of currency. Most currencies in operation right now are Fiat currencies, meaning they're currencies which are created and distributed by governments as the primary currency.

If there continues to be a worldwide question in terms of the legality and the regulation of cryptocurrencies, then it's unlikely that financial institutions will be adopting bitcoin and related cryptocurrencies any time soon, and it's equally unlikely that they're going to be integrating blockchain technology into their existing infrastructures.

That in and of itself is actually a huge question. A complete switch to blockchain would raise massive concerns of the viability of integration. Many financial institutions have infrastructures built from years upon years of experience and status quo currency and status quo financial transactions. Replacing these systems is no small feat at all.

In fact, it's so incredibly parallel that implementing blockchain on a large scale would largely require a massive and complete replacement of existing systems and infrastructure. This is honestly just a massive hurdle that would be nearly impossible to overcome.

On top of that, the fact is that the current state of affairs in the financial industry is - in a way - far more energy efficient than any possible blockchain implementation. Bitcoin mining, for example, takes a lot of energy. A lot of energy. Bitcoin miners, as of the time of writing, try around 450 thousand trillion solutions per second. That's a lot of processing power. That's an absurd amount of processing power. That processing power doesn't come out of thin air, either. Knowing financial institutions, that cost is likely to be remunerated by society.

Not to mention that the processing power required to drive such high frequency trading as, for example, the stock market, or the incredible number of financial transactions occurring every single second between people, would be insanely costly at first. Though this cost would be compensated in due time due to the nigh instant nature of blockchain transactions, it would be terribly costly up front to both procure the capital necessary for such a shift as well as override and replace existing financial infrastructure.

This isn't to say that it's totally impossible, but it would be an incredibly massive expense.

One of the last major hurdles in blockchain technology is its very nature. It requires people to not only be interested in the technology that it powers, but also interested and invested enough that they are willing to dedicate time and computing power to helping it grow. Its decentralized nature is as much of a curse as it is a blessing.

Blockchain, especially in its infancy, requires a culture in and of itself. It requires that people at large pick up the technology and not only accept the technology, but they go further and refuse to reject it. The difference between these is phenomenal. It's easy to accept and nurture a technology. It's harder to be an active fighter for it.

Blockchain is as incredibly prescient and powerful technology but the reality is that without adopters, it's not going to go anywhere.

Consider the blockchain ride sharing solutions that we talked about earlier, LaZooz and Arcade City. They're focused around their own cryptocurrencies and offering a decentralized ride sharing solution. That's all well and good, but what are those cryptocurrencies worth if there's nobody that wants them? What good are the decentralized ride sharing solutions worth if there's not a person on earth using the service? Clearly, this is a bit of hyperbole, but my point is that cultural adoption is not only necessary for these services to grow popular, but it's vital in order for them to succeed and bring blockchain technologies to their maximum potential.

This isn't to say that blockchain is a bad idea. Not at all. Blockchain is one of the most revolutionary technologies since the advent of the internet. I sincerely hope that I haven't given the impression that it's anything other than that. There are so many possibilities which opened up with the creation of decentralized consensus and the development of new peer to peer possibilities that don't have to be watched or guided by a third party intermediary. It's one of the boldest things to happen in technology in a long while.

But with that said, there are some very real and serious considerations that need to be made about blockchain and its possible applications and projects.

That said, I'm far from a naysayer. There are a great many people out there that actively try to deride and break down new technologies and horizons because they dislike the notion of changed. Whether from vested interest, general discomfort, or misplaced good intentions, these people will try to fearmonger and say that blockchain isn't worth the time or the investment. This isn't true. Blockchain has opened up so many doors in technology and will only open up more.

Any and all problems which present themselves are incredibly likely to have tangible solutions with time. For example, the security issue can be fixed by using advanced cryptography.

Moreover, those things which don't have direct fixes are innate limitations of the structure of the concept in the first place. These things largely were known and acknowledged since the invention of the blockchain, and the fact is that for things which are limited by these constraints, blockchain plain and simply may not be the absolute best solution.

While we're on that topic, we need to discuss when to use and when not to use blockchain.

Let's think one last time about what blockchain is and what it represents. A blockchain is just a database that has multiple manifestations and verification steps. But because of its nature, it's best suited to large operations that involve many users.

If your process or venture doesn't have the potential to have a great many people using and verifying the blocks, then it's likely that you're going to waste time implementing a blockchain solution when a database would serve you just as well for what you're needing.

Earlier, I said that many times when you're tempted to use a private blockchain, it'll be a waste of time. I still think this is true. There are numerous individuals who will disagree with me, but I think it's undeniable that blockchains that aren't completely decentralized are self-defeating. Thus, if you think that you'd like to implement a blockchain that can only be accessed and verified by certain nodes, it may be worth reviewing your project and determining whether a simple database would meet your needs just as well. Chances are that it will, and will be more efficient than the blockchain structure would be in such a case.

With all of that said, don't let me discourage you from trying to implement blockchains if you think they're a good idea or will benefit your venture. Just be aware that there are plenty of times that blockchains may not be the greatest idea for a given data set. Even if it's constantly expanding, that doesn't mean that blockchain is the best idea.

Blockchain works best for keeping a ledger of data transactions that are not corruptible and are desired to be immutable. Note that this isn't necessarily financial transactions - these are any transactions of data that are set in stone. Events of the past that are finite and complete and done. If your data set doesn't meet these criteria, you most likely will not want to implement a blockchain.

With those provisions in mind, it's time that we pull this book to a close. I feel bad for ending the book on these sort of downers, but I built blockchain up for 5 or so chapters, so it was necessary to instill some sort of caution. Blockchain is a type of technology. This means that it's imperfect, and this also means it isn't a jack of all trades. It has its niches and its applications, and though they may be manifold, you cannot and will not be able to meaningfully apply a blockchain to quite a few things.

Conclusion

Thank for making it through to the end of Blockchain: The Revolutionary Potential and Impact of Blockchain Technology in Businesses, Finances, and the World. Let's hope it was informative and able to provide you with all of the tools you need to achieve your goals whatever it may be.

The next step is to start dreaming. As cliché as that sounds, this technology truly has so many applications. If you're a creative person and you think you'd be interested in coming up with ideas and applications for blockchain technology then by all means, do it. This world needs innovators. This technology has the opportunity to change everything, and I'm of the firm belief that it's going to do exactly that.

Like any technology, it has its limits. There are very real concerns concerning blockchain technology and the limits of what it can accomplish, but these aren't finite and aren't going to vary in every application. For example, just because scalability presents a bounds that will be difficult to pass in terms of blockchain applicability in the financial sector, that same issue doesn't necessarily exist in operations where the blockchain has a fixed size that it will eventually reach. The infinite nature of financial transactions doesn't apply to events where a finite bounds is presented, such as the very nuanced electoral voting example that I gave earlier.

That is to say that there are many applications of blockchain that haven't been thought of yet. Many people tend to think of it as an infinite ledger for financial transaction, but in reality, that may not be where it shines.

Blockchain's defining features are its decentralization and its relatively corruption free and transparent nature. These are the things that make it shine as technology.

There are certainly applications to be discovered where decentralization and transparency are amicable features, and these are the things which need to be sought out. It's appealing for infinitely scaling peer-to-peer networks, but it's just as appealing for those applications we haven't figured out yet where its drawbacks are mitigated and its numerous feats and positive qualities are amplified and pronounced.

But regardless of whether your application mitigates the drawbacks or not, what's important is that you come up with an application of blockchain to fix something broken or corrupt.

Actually, let me take that further: what I'm saying here is that blockchain needs you. It needs thinkers that are willing to slave over ideas and churn out new applications for this fledgling technology. This world is full of so much corruption. Blockchain offers a way around it; blockchain offers true transparency in the face of otherwise questionable practices.

If you're not a techie, then you can still do your part by promoting existing blockchain services. Seek them out. There are a great many out there, and even more popping up every single day. You can invest in up-and-coming cryptocurrencies (or ones which already exist!) or spread the word about the latest decentralized peer to peer whatever-it-may-be. All that's important is that more people - as many people as possible - become aware of the revolutionary potential of this technology.

Finally, if you found this book useful in anyway, a review on Amazon is always appreciated!

www.ingramcontent.com/pod-product-compliance
Lightning Source LLC
Chambersburg PA
CBHW070719210526
45170CB00021B/1079